mac 200

Cartoons from the *Daily Mail*

Stan McMurtry **mac**
Edited by Mark Bryant

ROBSON BOOKS

For my grandchildren, Nick, Katie, Megan and Finlay.

First published in the United Kingdom in 2007 by
Robson Books
10 Southcombe Street
London
W14 0RA

An imprint of Anova Books Company Ltd

ISBN 10: 1 90579 815 6
ISBN 13: 9781905798155

A CIP catalogue record for this book is available from the British Library.

10 9 8 7 6 5 4 3 2 1

Typeset by SX Composing DTP, Rayleigh, Essex
Printed and bound by WS Bookwell, Finland

This book can be ordered direct from the publisher.
Contact the marketing department, but try your bookshop first.

www.anovabooks.com

Home Secretary John Reid revealed that though Britain had one of the highest crime rates in Europe only thirteen out of every 1000 offenders received prison sentences. Meanwhile, British Gas raised its prices for the third time in twelve months.

'I don't know what you've got to tut about so soon after connecting our gas supply to next door's meter." *28 July 2006*

A Scotland Yard inquiry leaked to the BBC revealed that more than 1000 prison officers accepted bribes and supplied mobile phones and drugs to inmates in British prisons.

'. . . so that's drugs, call girls, mobile phones and duplicate cell keys – American Express? That'll do nicely, sir.' *1 August*

As the conflict in the Middle East escalated, Tony Blair visited Los Angeles for a meeting on global warming with the Governor of California, Arnold Schwarzenegger, who jokingly offered him a part in *Terminator 4* when he left office.

'Try to relax, Tony. It's not good for you to be thinking about the Middle East all the time.' *2 August*

A 36-year-old City high-flyer at Deutsche Bank in London won more than £800,000 in damages after a six-year campaign of bullying by four of her female colleagues.

'Ah, Miss Wilkins. You're three hours late and drunk again. Time for a small pay rise we think.' *3 August*

As the Prime Minister sipped cocktails with pop stars on Sunset Strip and schmoozed with America's rich and famous, 70 civilians died in Iraq and four British soldiers were killed.

'I'm afraid I have some bad news about your son.' *4 August*

When the Foreign Secretary Margaret Beckett and her husband Leo took their summer holiday in a 23-foot caravan in France they were accompanied by three Special Branch officers.

'Tango, Victor, Foxtrot. Special Branch calling Foreign Secretary. All quiet so far, ma'am.' *8 August*

Police were called by a security guard at Sir Paul McCartney's mansion when the former Beatle's ex-wife, Heather Mills, tried to get in to the house after the locks had been changed.

'Your wife is here again, Sir Paul. Shall I release the piranha fish?' *9 August*

After the driest summer on record, a hosepipe ban and draconian drought measures were introduced. None the less a poll revealed that more than 750,000 householders in the South East were willing to risk a £1000 fine by watering their gardens at night.

'Psst, lads. Let's do a deal – I won't tell anybody if you don't.' *10 August*

As British police smashed a terrorist plot to mark the anniversary of the 2001 World Trade Center attack in New York, the Prime Minister denied that Britain's continued support of US action in Iraq made the country more vulnerable to terrorism.

'As ye sow, so shall ye reap.' *11 August*

Shortly after the Prime Minister and his family flew to the Caribbean for a holiday on the 62-foot luxury catamaran *Good Vibrations*, a huge security alert was imposed at British airports, cancelling hundreds of flights and affecting 500,000 passengers.

'Just think, Cherie. If I hadn't arranged a huge security alert these beaches would be absolutely swarming with people.' *15 August*

At an industrial tribunal in Southampton a gay policeman who had been disciplined for wearing a gold ear-stud accused Hampshire Constabulary of sexual discrimination when it allowed women to wear earrings on duty but not men.

'Dammit, constable! Are you trying to make us a laughing stock? You know the rules about wearing earrings.' *16 August*

Official police figures revealed that thefts at airports had increased greatly over the past twelve months. Meanwhile, almost a week after the security alert at Heathrow, British Airways admitted that 10,000 pieces of luggage were still missing.

'Hello, your dad's home with more bags nicked from Heathrow.' *17 August*

'Back again, Mr Prescott? How can I help you this time?' *18 August*

After being accused of ball-tampering, the Pakistan cricket team refused to resume play at the Oval Test Match against England, thereby forfeiting the game and losing the series.

'Okay, lads. Till they've sorted the ball-tampering allegation out, let's do some fielding practice . . . send the ball over here, Wazeem.' *22 August*

There was public amazement and disbelief when Metropolitan Police Commissioner Sir Ian Blair announced in a magazine interview that the capital is becoming so safe that residents are happy to leave their front doors open.

'All right. Which one of you left the outside door unlocked?' *23 August*

The National Farmers' Union and a number of academics backed claims made by West Country cheesemakers that cows moo with regional accents depending on which part of Britain they live in.

'Thanks for the elocution lessons but I think I preferred them mooing with a Brummie accent.' *24 August*

Department of Work & Pensions figures revealed that more than a million foreign migrants had registered for work in the UK in the past two years with thousands of Romanians and Bulgarians expected to increase the flood when they join the EU in 2007.

'Looks like the Government is preparing itself to get tough on future immigration.' *25 August*

In an attempt to encourage recycling, wheelie-bin 'spy bugs' were introduced in parts of Britain. The size of a 1p piece, the German-made bugs transmit information about the address of the house the bin belongs to and how much the rubbish weighs.

'Apparently when these new spy bugs detect unrecycled rubbish it activates a spring mechanism which returns it to the house.'
29 August

An article in *BBC History* magazine said that Margaret Thatcher had been Britain's most effective prime minister over the past 100 years. Meanwhile, a Harley Street doctor claimed that he had discovered an 'eternal youth' drug based on human growth hormones.

'. . . and I'm on the new "eternal youth" drug – you've got five minutes to pack!' *30 August*

Norwich Crown Court heard the case of a 38-year-old conman from Cambridgeshire who had faked letters of recommendation to receive an MBE from the Queen in 2003.

'We've already checked for conmen, ma'am. I think you'll find that one was genuine.' *31 August*

In an attempt to tackle the chronic shortage of organ donors, a new law was introduced to allow people to donate organs to those who are not relatives and to prevent families from overriding the wishes of the deceased who had registered as donors.

'You're far too generous with people coming to the door for donations – I expect that one cost you an arm and a leg.' *1 September*

A British gynaecological surgeon from Hammersmith Hospital, London, said that ground-breaking new research meant that womb transplants could be a reality within two years, giving new hope to infertile women.

'That's right, lover man. Instead of cosmetic surgery, I got me a womb transplant. Now I just need your contribution . . .' *5 September*

A 31-year-old Iraqi man who lost his sight in a bomb-blast in his homeland became the first blind person in the UK to be convicted of dangerous driving. Arrested in the West Midlands, he had been given instructions on braking and turning by a passenger.

'Okay, relax. It isn't that blind bloke driving again. It's his guide dog.' *6 September*

As the uncertainty continued over the date of Tony Blair's departure a leaked dossier by his personal adviser, Philip Gould, proposed appearances on *Blue Peter* and *Songs of Praise* and a farewell tour to celebrate the 'triumph of Blairism' which would leave 'the crowds wanting more'.

'Picture it, Gordon . . . the world is in mourning but then after three days I am resurrected. "Lo, he is risen." The multitude cry: "It's a miracle!" ' *7 September*

'Okay, for £150,000 is the answer (a) Your place, (b) My place, (c) Get lost, you drunken twit, or (d) Look out, here's your wife?'
12 September

Tony Blair made his last Labour Party Conference speech. Meanwhile, in an attempt to crack down on the huge increase in the domestic production of cannabis since its reclassification as a Class C drug, nineteen police forces raided addresses in England and Wales.

'Well, honestly. Blair's last conference speech and not a word about legalising cannabis factories to supplement pensions.'

27 September

A trial at the Old Bailey revealed that a 37-year-old Brazilian cleaner accused of blackmailing a 60-year-old judge with videos of him having sex with a female judge had herself also regularly had sex with him and had done his ironing and shopping.

'Thanks for the offer, Mrs Figgis. But let's just stick to cleaning, ironing and shopping for now, shall we?' *28 September*

Opposition MPs demanded that British troops serving in Iraq and Afghanistan should be given the same tax breaks as their foreign allies when it was pointed out that US troops are exempt from paying tax while stationed in a theatre of war.

'Young man. There appears to be a small discrepancy in your last tax return.' *3 October*

Critics of Environment Minister Ben Bradshaw's plans for 'pay-as-you-throw' charges based on the volume of refuse families discard – as calculated by wheelie-bin bugs – claimed that it would encourage fly-tipping and the dumping of rubbish into neighbours' bins.

'Stop worrying. Think of the money we'll save putting our rubbish in next door's wheelie bin.' *6 October*

A report published by Parliament's Public Accounts Committee revealed that early-release prisoners wearing electronic tags had committed more than 1000 violent offences – including murder and rape – since the scheme had been introduced.

'Yeah . . . nice, innit? It's Ron's tag. I get to wear it while he's out mugging people.' *13 October*

An employment tribunal found against a 24-year-old British-born Muslim teaching assistant in a Yorkshire primary school who had been sacked after insisting on wearing a full-face veil after she had been interviewed for the job without one.

'Good heavens, you're right, Miss Belcher! She's behind the bicycle sheds in a miniskirt having a fag.' *17 October*

There was a public outcry over 'cash for babies' when the 48-year-old US pop star Madonna flouted Malawi law and legal challenges from children's charities and aid groups to bring a 13-month-old boy she had adopted back to her home in the UK.

'Remember, son. When Madonna opens the door try to look appealing.' *18 October*

Bolton Crown Court heard how a 59-year-old former magistrate stole cash from the furniture store where he worked to pay a woman £200 an hour – eventually totalling more than £250,000 – to clean his house in the nude.

'Well, can't stop. I've got a job interview with that JP who lives up the road.' *25 October*

A 51-year-old accountant from Jersey launched a High Court battle to prove that he was Princess Margaret's 'secret son'. Born in Kenya, he believed he was the result of a liaison between the princess and either Group Captain Peter Townsend or Robin Douglas-Home.

'We are here to stay with Auntie Elizabeth and Uncle Philip – I am Princess Margaret's secret son, Igor.' *26 October*

Tory environment spokesman Greg Barker, married for fourteen years and with three children, split from his family after a homosexual affair with an interior designer who had been engaged to work on the couple's home in Rye, Sussex.

'Would you mind doing up your top buttons, Mr Wadkins? I don't want you giving my husband ideas.' *27 October*

In a major breakthrough in stem-cell research which could revolutionise the future of organ transplants, British scientists at Newcastle University announced that they had produced the world's first ever laboratory-grown human liver.

'Thanks for leaving me that bit of liver last night. It went down a treat with the onions and gravy.' *1 November*

The Queen opened the new session of Parliament. Meanwhile, in what many saw as another intrusion by the 'nanny state', the Government introduced a National Academy for Parenting Practitioners to make sure parents read and sang nursery rhymes to their young children.

'. . . and for any children listening, my Government have asked me to sing . . . Baa Baa Black Sheep Have You Any Wool . . .'

15 November

In a move that was condemned by many the Government proposed that 25 crimes – including theft, criminal damage, wasting police time and hoax calls to the fire service – would not incur charges if the perpetrators apologised for their actions.

'**Before we go, did everybody remember to say sorry?**' *16 November*

In his attempt to become the country's 'greenest' royal, Prince Charles told his aides to make more use of bicycles but at the same time refused to reduce his own personal car fleet which includes a Jaguar, a Range Rover and a classic 1969 Aston Martin.

'Can you pedal a bit faster, Camilla? I'm talking to an environmental group in half an hour.' *17 November*

A 55-year-old British Airways employee who had worn a tiny Christian cross around her neck to work for seven years took the airline to court over its new regulations which insisted that all personal items should be worn under the BA uniform.

'Y'know, British Airways are right. A cross does look better worn under the uniform.' *22 November*

In what many saw as a further extension of the 'Big Brother' culture, a new scheme was introduced in which all motorists pulled over by the police would be fingerprinted at the roadside to check their identity against the 6.5 million recorded prints of crime suspects.

'Good Lord, Marjorie. Is this true? Your prints match those found at the Brink's-Mat bullion heist 23 years ago.' *23 November*

In an attempt to reduce crime caused by drug addicts, trials were carried out to give hardcore junkies heroin on the NHS at a time when vital drugs for cancer and Alzheimer's sufferers were being denied by the Government.

'I'm just popping out to rob a few people to pay for your Alzheimer's drugs, dear.' *24 November*

To mark the bicentenary of the Slave Trade Abolition Act, the Prime Minister expressed his 'deep sorrow' at the sale of millions of Africans into slavery in the past.

'What's Blair apologising for? Slavery was abolished years ago.' *28 November*

When the cause of the mysterious death of KGB defector Alexander Litvinenko was eventually discovered to be poisoning by radioactive Polonium 210 there were suspicions that the Russian government itself was involved.

'Some incriminating evidence, Bert. Whoever put this bin out too early works for the Russian Embassy.' *29 November*

'Please understand, I don't do this just for the money, more for the buzz it gives me – ten years!' *30 November*

As it was revealed that the number of immigrants to Britain from Eastern Europe was at least sixteen times the original prediction of 13,000 a year, the Government launched a new Migration Advisory Committee to advise on the 'optimum level' of new arrivals.

'Blast! Every time a new batch of immigrants arrive in southern England, I have to buy a longer line.' *1 December*

MPs were reluctant to back Tony Blair's bid to replace Britain's nuclear taskforce with a new generation of Trident submarines but had no difficulty in supporting a move to increase their salaries to an average of £100,000 a year, a 66 per cent increase.

'Personally, I say to hell with Trident. We should spend the money keeping this trough filled.' *5 December*

There was widespread disbelief from doctors' leaders, health campaigners and unions when the Government announced that its plan to close down one in four Accident & Emergency departments in Britain's hospitals would actually improve patient care.

'If they've closed the next casualty hospital too, Hoskins, just switch your wipers on.' *6 December*

A report in the journal *Science* published striking new images of Mars which seemed to suggest that water had been flowing on its surface in recent years. Meanwhile, water companies in Britain continued to be criticised for wastage through pipeline leaks.

'Bills, bills, bills! But when are you going to do something about these leaks? I expect they can be seen for miles.' *8 December*

During the preparation for a retrospective of the work of the artist Euan Uglow it was revealed that Cherie Blair had posed, half-naked, for his painting entitled *Striding Nude, Blue Dress* in 1978 when she was a 24-year-old law student.

'Are you sending any personal Christmas cards to your barrister friends this year, Cherie?'

12 December

The 'cash-for peerages' case took a new turn when Tony Blair himself was questioned by police over four Labour Party lenders who had received seats in the House of Lords after being personally recommended by the Prime Minister.

'If we do meet the Blessed One, are you sure this'll be enough for a peerage each?' *19 December*

Speaking to the Council of Foreign Relations think-tank in New York, Iraq's Vice-President Tareq Al-Hashemi claimed that Tony Blair had set a timetable for pulling British troops out of Iraq but that George Bush had 'brainwashed' him into changing his mind.

'Gee, George, honey. Why's Tony doing backward flips outside Downing Street in his underpants?' *21 December*

'Those were his last words – "Ho, ho, ho. Happy Christmas, everybody. . ."' *22 December*

With thousands of pubs serving alcohol until the early hours of the morning under the new 24-hour licensing laws the festive season heralded the worst ever cases of binge drinking.

'Yes, thank you. I've had a lovely Christmas break – and I'd like to apologise for Sellotaping you to your chair at the office party.'

3 January 2007

In an interview for the BBC a British Army general admitted that, despite £700 million being spent on improvements to services' housing last year, many soldiers and their families still lived in dilapidated and outdated accommodation.

'Your leave is nearly over, darling. I bet you're dreading going back to Iraq.' *5 January*

When paparazzi and TV camera crews began to dog the footsteps of Kate Middleton following rumours of her forthcoming engagement to Prince William, the prince himself intervened to urge the media to give his girlfriend some privacy.

'Alone at last, Kate, darling.' *10 January*

There were more fears about 'Frankenstein Farming' when it was revealed that Dundee Paradise, the calf of a black-and-white cow cloned in a US laboratory from cells taken from the ear of a champion dairy Holstein, had been born in the UK.

'Yeah. Hard to believe, isn't it? In the early years of experimental cloning us girls were content to just chew grass and get milked.' *11 January*

A report by the Commission for Social Care said that the Welfare State was no longer able to give free help to the frail and elderly. Meanwhile, the Home Office claimed it knew nothing of crimes committed by Britons abroad.

'Oh, come along! Lots of people are old, confused and can't remember anything, but they still go out to work at the Home Office.' *12 January*

As Victoria Beckham looked for a new home in Hollywood following the £128 million signing of her husband to play for the LA Galaxy football team, Tony Blair was criticised for taking a freebie New Year holiday at pop star Robin Gibb's Miami mansion.

'I'm sorry, this one won't do either – Tony Blair says he thinks the guest suite sounds a bit small.' *16 January*

Dame Helen Mirren won the award for Best Actress at Hollywood's Golden Globe Awards for her role in the film *The Queen* about the life of Elizabeth II.

'How terribly exciting, Philip, dear. They're making a film called *Helen Mirren* and I've been offered the part.' *17 January*

After a long, dry summer with widespread hosepipe bans, Britain experienced its worst storms for 17 years, with torrential rain, winds up to 99 miles per hour and more than 100,000 homes left without electricity as power lines were torn down.

'His last words were: "Look on the bright side, the hosepipe ban has been lifted."' *19 January*

When the container ship MSC *Napoli* ran aground on Branscombe Beach in Devon hundreds of looters made off with wine barrels, perfume, BMW motorbikes and other goods washed ashore from the stricken vessel.

'Doris, it's me. Can I borrow a tin-opener?' *23 January*

To alleviate Britain's overcrowded jails a letter signed by the Home Secretary, Lord Chancellor and Attorney-General was sent to all courts in the UK requesting magistrates to imprison only the most dangerous criminals and to give early release to those with sentences of twelve months or less.

'Dammit, Higgins, Let go! You're being released early whether you like it or not!' *26 January*

A retired administrator from a Spanish chain store became the world's oldest mother when she gave birth to twins in Barcelona just ten days before her 67th birthday after receiving treatment from a fertility clinic in Los Angeles.

'We have a problem. The baby was born, took one look at his mother then went back in again.' *30 January*

Culture, Media & Sport Secretary, Tessa Jowell, pressed ahead with her controversial plans to launch Britain's first supercasino despite widespread concern that it would expose thousands of vulnerable people to exploitation and the misery of debt.

'No mate. This is going to be the new super pawn shop. The casino is being built next door.' *31 January*

In an effort to contain an outbreak of the virulent version of bird flu which had been detected at Bernard Matthews's turkey farm in Suffolk, 160,000 turkeys were slaughtered and 535 farms in East Anglia were sealed off to protect the British poultry industry.

'Left, left . . . straighten up a bit . . . we're wobbling . . . okay, forward . . .' *6 February*

Shocking figures from the new *European Crime and Safety Survey*, the most comprehensive analysis of crime, security and safety ever conducted in the EU, revealed that Britain is Europe's burglary capital.

'Lock the front door, Harold. It says on telly that Britain is the most burgled place in Europe.' *7 February*

British Airways introduced new regulations that allowed passengers to
check in only one bag with a maximum weight of 23 kilograms.
Additional luggage would be charged at £120 per bag.

'Yes, just the one bag, thank you.' *9 February*

A new biography of Conservative Party leader David Cameron revealed that he had been disciplined at Eton for smoking cannabis at the age of 15.

'Dashed if I know what Cameron saw in this stuff. Does nothing for me . . . my God, you're beautiful!' *13 February*

As couples across the country exchanged romantic gifts a survey revealed that 54% of British women can't stand Valentine's Day.

'Those Valentine sweets you brought me were so nice, darling. I ate the lot. What were they?' *14 February*

As London Fashion Week began, the death of another young catwalk model suspected of suffering from anorexia triggered further international debate about the use of 'size-zero' models in fashion shows.

'Dammit, Lucinda. I told you to watch where you walk. That dress was worth £6000!' *16 February*

Consumer groups accused banking-industry leaders of 'pure greed' when they announced that they would soon scrap free banking and introduce monthly fees on current accounts at a time when they had just unveiled record annual profits of £40 billion.

'Keep your distance, lads. That's the new gang in town – they're called bank managers.' *21 February*

Despite the security nightmare it created, 22-year-old Prince Harry insisted that he wished to accompany his regiment, the Blues & Royals, on their forthcoming six-month tour of duty in Iraq.

'I'm sorry, your Royal Highness. But it's the only way your gran will let you go.' *23 February*

The *Daily Mail* began a campaign to lobby for the Government to provide drugs on the NHS to treat Alzheimer's Disease (which affects 400,000 in the UK) rather than spend it on marketing consultants and free heroin for junkies.

'There are times when I wish I could forget the last ten years under Tony Blair.' *28 February*

Scientists at the Robot Engineering Technology Research Centre at the Shandong University of Science & Technology in China claimed to have used microchips implanted in pigeons' brains to create the world's first remote-controlled birds.

'Me too. I was going to settle on a statue but had this strange urge to come in here.' *1 March*

Thousands of motorists in the south-east of England were hit by breakdowns caused by contaminated fuel supplied by supermarkets.

'Hurry up, man. We're in the middle of a police chase!' *2 March*

In an attempt to get 300,000 single parents back to work and off state benefits, Chancellor Gordon Brown announced measures to force them to seek work when their youngest child reached the age of 12 rather than the current age of 16.

'Sorry, Mum, we can't look under 12 for ever – you'll have to find a job.' *5 March*

In another 'Frankenstein food' case which British watchdog officials described as 'very disturbing', a California-based company was given US government approval to grow test crops of rice which had been genetically modified with human DNA.

'Aaaaaaaaaaaaaaaaaaaargh!' *7 March*

After the inquiry into the 'cash-for-peerages' scandal heard that Labour fundraiser Lord Levy, known as 'Lord Cashpoint', had tried to bully No. 10's Director of Government Relations into changing her story, it seemed that he would soon be charged.

'I'm sorry, Lord Levy is out right now. I don't know when he'll be back.' *8 March*

NHS consultants threatened to revolt when a new computer system designed to advertise vacancies for junior doctors could not handle 30,000 applications for 20,000 jobs and many well qualified candidates were not invited for interview.

'Do we have a deal? A full health check for me and that job stacking shelves at Tesco is as good as yours.' *9 March*

Tony Blair's new 'security, crime and justice' policy review, outlining his vision for the next decade, said that all schoolchildren should be monitored for criminal tendencies.

'I must warn you, Pickering. Tony Blair has decreed that all children are to be monitored for signs of criminal behaviour.'

28 March

In a landmark High Court case, judges ruled that a businessman did not have to pay a £50 parking fine because he had driven away before the traffic warden had placed the ticket on his car.

'Okay. He's nearly finished writing the ticket – jam on the brakes.' *29 March*

Shortly before he was due to be posted to Iraq, 22-year-old Prince Harry was reprimanded by superior officers in his regiment, the Blues & Royals, after a series of incidents in which he was found to be drunk and disorderly in public places.

'Oh really? Well I brought my granny along too and we both think your conduct has been appalling!' *3 April*

Radio and TV presenters accused the BBC of ageism and sexism when 55-year-old Moira Stuart was axed from her job as newsreader. Meanwhile, soon after his infidelity had ended his marriage, Chris Tarrant was revealed to have a new partner.

'What a protest! John Humphrys, Trevor McDonald, Michael Buerk, Sue MacGregor and ooh look . . . Chris Tarrant.' *4 April*

In an interview published in *NME*, 63-year-old Rolling Stones guitarist Keith Richards revealed that he had once mixed his father's ashes with cocaine and inhaled them.

'I've got some bad news for you, son. I've asked to be buried.' *5 April*

After almost a fortnight of captivity, seven British sailors and eight Royal Marines held hostage for allegedly straying into Iranian waters whilst on patrol in Iraq, were released, dressed in civilian clothes supplied by the Iranian government.

'Not only has it been a wonderful propaganda coup, gentlemen, but Blair has promised to send the suits back by Wednesday.'

6 April

There was widespread condemnation by former Defence Ministers, ex-service personnel and relatives of those who had died in Iraq and Afghanistan when the Ministry of Defence allowed the former Iranian hostages to sell their stories to the media.

End of Story – For Some *10 April*

In a move that was seen by many as creating a 'charter for yobs', Education Secretary Alan Johnson unveiled new guidelines for tackling soaring indiscipline in schools by forcing teachers to reward disruptive pupils with prizes and privileges.

'Doesn't it make you proud, Ron? Our Wayne has been made head boy of the school he burned down.' *11 April*

Only months after Kate Middleton's appearance at Prince William's graduation parade at Sandhurst had led to speculation about their engagement, it was announced that their four-year relationship was over.

'Romantic guy. Tall, good-looking. Seeks fun-loving chick who enjoys parties, polo, rugby and is not averse to walking around with a big heavy crown on her head.' *17 April*

To cope with the coffins of ever larger men and women it was revealed that some British crematoria had begun to import supersize furnaces from the USA, which has the world's highest rates of obesity.

'. . . And now a prayer for the pallbearers, four of whom have had heart attacks and the other two hernias . . .' *19 April*

The pop singer Madonna was rumoured to be about to adopt a 3-year-old girl from an orphanage in Malawi. Meanwhile, farmer Bernard Matthews was awarded £600,000 in compensation for the culling of his flock of turkeys during the bird-flu scare.

'Things are looking up here. There's a rumour that one of my chicks is up for adoption by Madonna.' *20 April*

A report by a Fellow of the British Psychological Society claimed that watching too much TV leads to obesity and heart disease in children. Meanwhile, 144 councils in England and Wales introduced fortnightly refuse collections.

'Personally I blame fortnightly rubbish collections.' *25 April*

Astronomers at the La Silla observatory in the Chilean Andes discovered a new planet in the constellation of Libra, more than twenty light years away, which has a remarkable similarity to Earth.

'Read orl abaht it . . . dustbins to be emptied twice a year . . . council tax to double . . . new planet discovered just like ours called Earth.' *26 April*

In an attempt to combat unnecessary waste a number of supermarkets announced that they would no longer give away free plastic carrier-bags while others set up huge wheelie bins in their stores for customers to dump packaging and food wrappings.

'Damn! I don't think you'll be having soup tonight.' *27 April*

On the tenth anniversary of the General Election which swept Tony Blair to power, the Prime Minister said that he would formally announce his resignation the following week and would officially endorse Gordon Brown as his successor.

2 May

Lord Browne of Madingley, known as the 'Sun King of Oil' for his success as chief executive of BP, was forced to resign in disgrace after being found guilty of perjury in an attempt to deny claims made by his former gay lover.

'Lord Browne's come to clear his desk – not having a very good week, is he?' *3 May*

In the local council elections the Labour Party suffered its worst defeat in 35 years. Amongst the casualties were many of the Labour-run local authorities which had introduced fortnightly refuse collections.

'Now they've been voted out, do we collect them this week or in a fortnight?' *4 May*

As Tony Blair prepared to leave No.10 many thought his wife's performance with *Strictly Come Dancing* star Anton du Beke at a charity ball left much to be desired.

'That's agreed then? A huge clap of thunder, a bolt of lightning, then written in the sky: "Behold my servant departeth on 27 June, memoirs out soon priced £20".' *8 May*

At a historic ceremony in Stormont Castle, Belfast, the Rev. Ian Paisley, leader of the Democratic Unionist Party, became First Minister of Northern Ireland's new devolved power-sharing government with Sinn Fein's Martin McGuiness as his deputy.

New Friends? *9 May*

While being shown round the Goddard Space Flight Center in Maryland on the last day of the Queen's state visit to the USA, Prince Philip asked an astronaut how he coped with performing natural bodily functions while in space.

'I'm so glad we spoke to those astronauts – this'll save me having to get up in the night.' *10 May*

Gordon Brown pledged that when he became Prime Minister one of his first tasks would be to force family doctors to restore proper out-of-hours care for their patients or risk a cut to their six-figure salaries.

'Roger has reached a compromise with Gordon Brown over longer hours. He's bringing some of his work home.' *15 May*

While dining with a TV producer in the MemSaab Indian restaurant in Nottingham, TV presenter Chris Tarrant was arrested on charges of assault after throwing a spoon at an overenthusiastic fan who continually pestered him.

'Not been your night, has it? First Chris Tarrant and then Uri Geller.' *16 May*

José Mourinho, 44-year-old Portuguese manager of Chelsea Football Club, was arrested and cautioned after hiding his pet Yorkshire Terrier from quarantine officers who believed he had brought the dog into the country illegally.

'We're having to do an urgent rabies test on this one. He bit two of our police officers.' *17 May*

The head of the British Army, General Sir Richard Dannatt, ruled that Prince Harry could not serve in Iraq as he would be a prime target for snipers and hostage-takers. There were suggestions that he might serve in Afghanistan instead.

'Well, chaps, here we are. Front line, Afghanistan and . . . oh, good shot, your Royal Highness!' *18 May*

A new Infrastructure Planning Commission was set up by Communities Secretary Ruth Kelly to steamroller through objections by 'Nimby' protesters to a new generation of nuclear power stations, airports, motorways and incineration plants.

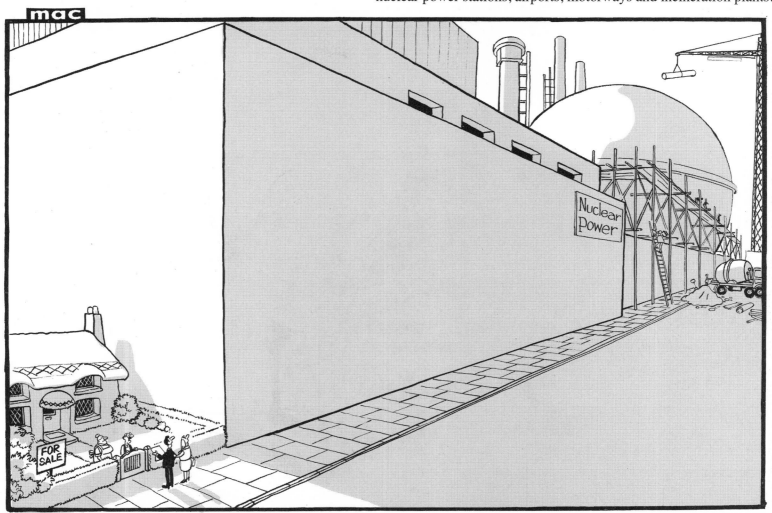

'No, we didn't put it in the Home Information Pack – they only put it up last night.' *22 May*

The Government revealed new plans to introduce no less than five separate recycling bins for householders to sort their rubbish into paper, cardboard, plastic, glass and food scraps or face penalties.

'Of course, recycling in a small, top-floor flat is very difficult. But we do our best . . . more cake, anyone?' *25 May*

Channel 4 television chiefs were accused of 'trampling on Princess Diana's grave' by proposing to broadcast the documentary *Diana: The Witnesses in the Tunnel* featuring paparazzi photos of her last moments in the Paris car crash of 1997.

'This script is sensitive, intelligent, witty and good clean family entertainment – you're fired!' *29 May*

Tony Blair's 'farewell tour' of the world reached Africa where he visited Libya, Sierra Leone and South Africa and used the occasion to rally the world's richest countries to help ease the plight of the poor and hungry in these nations.

'I liked that bit about helping the hungry in Africa . . . I was famished.' *30 May*

There was a public outcry over a new Dutch reality TV quiz show in which a woman, supposedly dying of cancer, offered a kidney to one of three contestants currently on dialysis. It was later revealed to be a hoax to highlight the shortage of organs for transplant.

'Guess what? I put your name down for a Dutch TV quiz programme.' *31 May*

At the annual conference of the British Medical Association it was proposed that family doctors should reopen their surgeries in the evenings, at weekends and during Bank Holidays for a fee of £20 per appointment.

'It's getting late. The doctor will see one more patient . . . £20 I'm bid . . . do I hear £30?' *5 June*

Despite receiving an official letter of protest written on behalf of Prince William and Prince Harry, Channel 4 went ahead with the broadcast of the documentary *Diana: The Witnesses in the Tunnel*.

'**Straight on, then second left and Channel 4 is on the right, Your Royal Highness.**' *6 June*

Fertility expert Professor Robert Winston of Imperial College, London University, told a conference that research had discovered a protein that could extend the life of women's eggs and that a new pill might soon be developed to delay the menopause.

'Come along, George. I've delayed the menopause long enough. It's time to have babies!" *12 June*

Communities Secretary Ruth Kelly introduced a Single Equalities Bill which proposed new laws to allow nursing mothers to breastfeed their babies in public with fines of up to £2500 for restaurants, cafés and shops which tried to ban them.

'Well, I think she should've wiggled her tassels and then fed them.' *13 June*

While being mobbed by a crowd of well-wishers in a farming village twenty miles from Tirana, capital of Albania, US President George Bush had his watch stolen.

'Godammit. This is the second time! Who's got mah watch?' *14 June*

Doctors and patients' groups condemned the Government's National Institution for Health and Clinical Excellence for allowing expensive sight-saving drugs to be available on the NHS in Scotland but not in England and Wales.

'Scotland!' *15 June*

The latest figures published by the Healthcare Commission watchdog as part of its annual 'health check' revealed that a quarter of the 394 English NHS Trusts had breached the Hygiene Code for hospitals introduced last October.

'Nurse! The rats have got old Ferguson again!' *19 June*

Effigies of the Queen were burnt in Pakistan and an Iranian group offered a bounty of £80,000 for the head of Salman Rushdie when the author of *The Satanic Verses* was granted a knighthood in the Queen's Birthday Honours list.

'Thank you for the offer, but when the time comes I must limit myself to gently tapping the sword on Mr Rushdie's shoulder.'

21 June

The Wimbledon tennis tournament got off to a tense start as Britain's Naomi Cavaday narrowly failed to win two match points against 1997 champion Martina Hingis. Meanwhile, Tony Blair finally resigned as Prime Minister and was succeeded by Gordon Brown.

'Gentlemen. Her Majesty doesn't want to be disturbed right now . . . but there is a message.' *27 June*

At his last Prime Minister's Question Time, Tony Blair was given an unprecedented standing ovation by Labour and Tory MPs. Meanwhile, a monsoon-like downpour led to widespread flooding as more rain fell in 24 hours than the average for the whole of June.

'. . . and so, as a fitting end to his ten glorious years, Tony Blair walks triumphantly off into the sunset . . .' *28 June*

Despite the fact that a huge piece of falling masonry had recently narrowly missed hitting Princess Anne's car, Buckingham Palace was told that there would be no increase to the annual public grant of £15 million for maintaining Britain's crumbling royal palaces.

'Yes, Mr Brown. More falling masonry . . . my husband has just gone up to inspect the damage.' *29 June*

It was the wettest June since records began 93 years ago with widespread flooding, especially in Yorkshire. Meanwhile, England finally followed the rest of the UK and imposed a smoking ban in pubs, restaurants, offices, factories and taxis on 1 July.

'I feel sorry for smokers. It must be freezing out there.' *3 July*

Two NHS doctors were among five people held as terror suspects after a series of bomb plots in London and at Glasgow Airport.

'Before you start, Bernard. Are you absolutely sure all NHS doctors are terrorists?' *4 July*

Wimbledon tennis officials faced a desperate battle to clear the worst backlog of matches for 25 years as rain, thunder, lightning and hailstones disrupted play. One match even lasted five days, the longest in the history of the tournament.

'Sorry to get you out of bed but it suddenly stopped raining and we're running well behind schedule.' *5 July*

There was considerable speculation that the publication of *The Blair Years*, the diaries of former Labour Party spin-doctor Alistair Campbell, would shed light on the sometimes stormy relationship between Tony Blair and his Chancellor, Gordon Brown.

'Oh dear. Looks like Gordon Brown's been talking to God, too.' *10 July*

A 20-year-old Muslim woman juror was thrown off a murder trial at Blackfriars Crown Court in London and faced contempt-of-court charges when it was discovered that she had been listening to an MP3 music player under her headscarf.

'Thank you for sharing with us the weather forecast, the right time and the top ten hits in Somalia – now can we have guilty or not guilty?' *11 July*

As Labour's Ken Livingstone, well known for his love of newts, approached the end of his four-year period as Mayor of London, it was announced that the colourful MP for Henley, Boris Johnson, would stand against him as the official Tory candidate.

'There's a newt at the door canvassing for Ken Livingstone.' *17 July*